Spring Diver

Spring Diver

Distinctive Specialty Course for PADI Instructors

Distinctive Specialty Course Instructor Guide

Spring Diver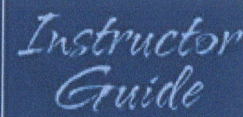

Copyright © 2018
by Edward Krawczyk and Edward Zellem

All rights reserved. With the permission of the copyright owners, items in this publication may be reproduced by PADI Members for use in PADI-sanctioned training. No part of this product may be stored in a retrieval system, or transmitted, in any form or by any means, electronic, mechanical, photocopying, recording or otherwise, without prior permission.

Published in the United States of America

Developed by
Edward Krawczyk
PADI Course Director #60038
and
Edward Zellem
PADI Master Scuba Diver Trainer #389640

ISBN-13: 978-0986238659
ISBN-10: 0986238651

Spring Diver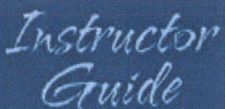

Table of Contents

Introduction

How to Use This Guide... 4
Course Philosophy and Goals.. 4
Course Flow Options.. 5

Section One: Course Standards

Standards at a Glance... 6
Instructor Prerequisites.. 7
Student Diver Prerequisites.. 7
Supervision and Ratios... 7
Site, Depths and Hours... 8
Materials and Equipment.. 9
Assessment Standards, Certification Requirements and Procedures................ 9

Section Two: Knowledge Development

Conduct.. 11
Learning Objectives... 12
Knowledge Development Teaching Outline.. 12
    Course Introduction... 13
    Course Goals and Overview.. 13
    Certification.. 14
    Class Requirements.. 14
    Course Content.. 15

Section Three: Open Water Dives

Confined Water Assessments or Training (Optional)..................................... 27
Open Water Dives Conduct... 28
Open Water Guidelines for Spring Diver... 29
Performance Requirements... 31
    Dive One... 31
    Dive Two... 32

Appendix

Spring Diver Knowledge Review Student Handout 38
Spring Diver Quick Review Answer Sheet... 50
Spring Diver Quick Review Answer Key.. 53
Specialty Training Record for Spring Diver.. 56

Spring Diver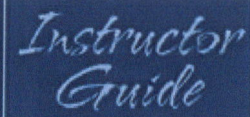

Introduction

How to Use this Guide

This guide is written for you, the PADI Spring Diver Distinctive Specialty Instructor. The guide contains three sections and an Appendix. The first section contains standards specific to this course, the second section contains knowledge development presentations, and the third section considers confined water training (optional) and details performance requirements for the open water dives. The Appendix includes a knowledge development handout that you may choose to provide to students for self-study, and a Quick Review to assess their understanding and retention.

All required standards, learning objectives, activities, and performance requirements specific to the PADI Spring Diver Distinctive Specialty Diver course appear in **boldface print. The boldface assists you in easily identifying those requirements that you *must* adhere to when you conduct the course.** Items not in boldface print are recommendations for your information and consideration. General course standards applicable to all PADI courses are located in the General Standards and Procedures section of your PADI *Instructor Manual*.

Course Philosophy and Goals

The purpose of the PADI Spring Diver Distinctive Specialty Diver course is to provide an introduction to freshwater spring diving: a fun and enjoyable form of diving that offers an alternative to saltwater and offshore diving. Springs are typically easy to access by car, inexpensive to dive in, and can offer inland divers many opportunities for fun and training that would otherwise require long-distance travel to the ocean. Spring diving also provides access to unique underwater ecosystems and geography that can be very different from saltwater diving.

The goals of the PADI Spring Diver Distinctive Specialty Diver course are to familiarize divers with the skills, knowledge, planning, organization, procedures, techniques, problems, hazards and enjoyment of spring diving. The overall goal is to provide a safe and supervised introduction to spring diving that will help divers discover and explore new opportunities underwater, regardless of their experience level. As always, training should emphasize safety and fun.

Spring Diver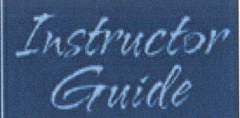

Course Flow Options

This course contains knowledge development and assessment, an optional confined water skills development and assessment session, and two open water training dives. When possible, you should conduct the knowledge development and assessment session *before* any open water training. However, knowledge development and assessment may be conducted at any point during the course. A student handout and Quick Review are included in the *Appendix* of this manual for your use as appropriate.

Confined water and/or surface practice sessions are not required for the Spring Diver Distinctive Specialty course; however, you may choose to have practical sessions that allow student divers to practice skills such as neutral buoyancy, finning techniques, and float/dive flag use. A general water skills assessment may also be appropriate if a student's diving capabilities are unknown to you, or if a student has not been diving for a long period of time. If a confined water skill session is included, it must precede the open water training dives.

There are two open water dives to complete and one knowledge development session. You may rearrange skill sequences within each dive, however the sequence of dives must stay intact. You may add more dives as necessary to meet student divers' needs or desires. Organize your course to incorporate environmentally friendly techniques throughout each dive, and to accommodate student divers' learning styles, logistical needs, and your sequencing preferences.

Spring Diver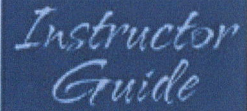

Section One: Course Standards

This section includes the course standards, recommendations, and suggestions for conducting the PADI Spring Diver Distinctive Specialty course.

Standards at a Glance

Topic	Course Standard
Minimum Instructor Rating	PADI Spring Diver Distinctive Specialty Instructor
Prerequisites Minimum Age	PADI (Junior) Open Water Diver 10 years
Ratios	**Open Water: 8:1 Instructor; 4:1 Certified Assistant. If children aged 10-11 participate: 4:1 with no more than two children aged 10-11 in the group. This ratio cannot increase by adding a certified assistant.**
Site, Depths and Hours	Depth: 9-24 metres/20-80 feet recommended • **Junior Open Water Diver: 9-12 metres/20-40 feet** • **Open Water Diver: 9-18 metres/20-60 feet** • Advanced Open Water Diver: 9-24 metres/20-80 feet Hours recommended: 12 **Minimum Open Water Dives: 2 dives** (2 different springs recommended)
Materials and Equipment	Instructor: • **PADI Spring Diver Distinctive Specialty Instructor Guide** • Lines, reels, floats, flags, knife/diver tools capable of cutting line, lights, other equipment as needed for spring diving in the local environment, spare parts kit, extra weight in small increments for student trim

Spring Diver

Instructor Prerequisites

To qualify to teach the PADI Spring Diver Distinctive Specialty course, an individual must be a Teaching status PADI Open Water Scuba Instructor or higher. PADI Instructors may apply for the Spring Diver Distinctive Specialty Instructor rating after completing a Specialty Instructor Training course with a PADI Course Director, or by providing proof of experience and applying directly to PADI. For further detail, reference Specialty Instructor in the Professional Membership section of your PADI *Instructor Manual*.

Student Diver Prerequisites

By the start of the course, a diver must be:
1. **Certified as a PADI (Junior) Open Water Diver or have a qualifying certification from another training organization.** In this case, a qualifying certification is defined as proof of entry-level scuba certification with a minimum of four open water training dives. Verify student diver prerequisite skills and provide remediation as necessary.

2. **At least 10 years old.**

Supervision and Ratios

Open Water Dives

A Teaching Status PADI Spring Diver Distinctive Specialty Instructor must be present and in control of all activities. If any dive is deeper than 18 meters/60 feet, the Distinctive Specialty Instructor must directly supervise at a ratio of no greater than 8 students per instructor (8:1). Otherwise, the Distinctive Specialty Instructor may indirectly supervise all dives. The Distinctive Specialty Instructor must ensure that all performance requirements are met.

The ratio for open water dives is 8 student divers per instructor (8:1), with 4 additional student divers allowed per certified assistant (4:1). If children aged 10-11 participate: 4:1 with no more than two children aged 10-11 in the group. This ratio cannot increase by adding a certified assistant.

During open water training dives, do not allow student divers to enter an overhead environment where direct vertical access to the surface is not possible.

Spring Diver

Site, Depths, and Hours

Site
Choose sites with conditions and environments suitable for completing requirements. Shallow dives will provide divers with more time to complete tasks and experience freshwater spring environments. If possible, use different open water dive sites to give student divers experience in dealing with logistical challenges in a variety of environmental conditions while incorporating environmentally friendly techniques throughout each dive.

Due to the potential for creating silty bottom conditions in some springs, student divers should be exposed or reintroduced to techniques and procedures for neutral buoyancy, proper weighting, and appropriate finning near sensitive bottom areas. You may elect to practice skills in confined water sessions first to better prepare divers to apply these skills in open water later.

Depths
9-24 metres/20-80 feet recommended.
- **Junior Open Water Diver: 9-12 metres/20-40 feet**
- **Open Water Diver: 9-18 metres/20-60 feet**
- Advanced Open Water Diver: 9-24 metres/20-80 feet

Always ensure maximum depths are consistent with student certification levels.

Hours
The PADI Spring Diver Distinctive Specialty course includes two open water dives, which may be conducted in one day. Conduct no more than three dives in one day. The minimum number of recommended hours is 12.

Spring Diver

Materials and Equipment

Instructor Materials and Equipment
Use the PADI Spring Diver Distinctive Specialty course materials prescriptively to accommodate various sequencing preferences and teaching and learning styles.

Required
- **PADI *Spring Diver Distinctive Specialty Course Instructor Guide***
- **Emergency Action Plan for spring dive site**

Recommended
- Specialty equipment needed to perform spring dives in the local environment.
- Lines, reels, floats or flags of different types as examples for students.
- Knife/diver tool capable of cutting lines.
- First aid kit, emergency O2 kit (if unavailable at dive site) and "Save-a-dive" kit.
- Primary and backup lights (if appropriate for local environment), typically for instructor's use only. <u>In general, students should be discouraged from carrying lights in the PADI Spring Diver Distinctive Specialty course if there is any chance of straying into an overhead environment</u>. This helps encourage students to remain in natural light zones, and to not enter any overhead or cavern environments without direct vertical access to the surface.
- The PADI *Encyclopedia of Recreational Diving*, Chapter 2, p. 2-59 to 2-62.

Assessment Standards
To assess knowledge, you should discuss the Learning Objectives found in Section 2 of this manual with students and then apply the Quick Review to evaluate understanding and retention. Student divers must demonstrate accurate and adequate knowledge during the open water dives and must perform all skills (both procedures and motor skills) fluidly, with little difficulty, in a manner that demonstrates minimal or no stress.

Spring Diver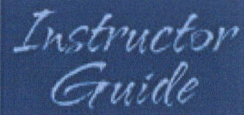

Certification Requirements and Procedures

Document student diver training by completing the Specialty Training Record for Spring Diver found in the Appendix. To qualify for certification, by the completion of the course student divers must complete a knowledge review session, the Spring Diver Quick Review, and all performance requirements for PADI Spring Diver Distinctive Specialty Course Open Water Dives One and Two.

The instructor certifying the student diver must ensure that all certification requirements have been met. The certifying instructor obtains a PADI Spring Diver Distinctive Specialty certification for students by submitting a completed, signed PIC to the appropriate PADI office. Reference the "Administrative Procedures of the General Standards and Procedures" section of your PADI *Instructor Manual* for detailed and additional information. The PADI Spring Diver Distinctive Specialty certification can be counted as one of the five specialty ratings required for a PADI Master Scuba Diver rating.

Spring Diver

Section Two: Knowledge Development

Conduct

The philosophy of this course is to focus on the skills, techniques and equipment that divers need to safely maximize their dives in freshwater springs, and to help divers achieve a better appreciation and understanding of spring environments.

There is one knowledge development session required. Work hand-in-hand with student divers to clarify and prescriptively address student diver misconceptions, and to enhance learning with respect to local practices, aquatic environments, and individual student interest. If there is a need for instructor-led presentations, use the following teaching outline, which appears in point form, as a road map of the conduct, content, sequence and structure for the PADI Spring Diver Distinctive Specialty course. You also should provide students with the Student Handout and Quick Review in the *Appendix* of this guide.

By the end of this program, you should have equipped student divers with the knowledge and experience needed to adapt what they've learned in this course to future spring diving adventures. The result should be student divers with both theoretical knowledge and practical experience who can adapt what they have learned to diving in any appropriate spring.

Regardless of how you conduct Knowledge Development, student divers will be able to explain the following Learning Objectives:

Spring Diver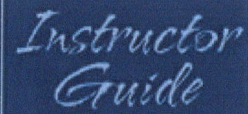

Knowledge Development

Learning Objectives
By the end of knowledge development, student divers will be able to explain:

Reasons why people spring dive, and its advantages and disadvantages.
- What is spring diving?
- What are four advantages of spring diving?
- What are five concerns of spring diving?

Spring diving environments.
- What is a spring?
- How are springs formed?
- What is an aquifer?
- What is karst?
- Explain the different types and classifications of springs.
- What are the characteristics of springs?
- What is a thermocline? What is a halocline? What is their relationship to spring diving?

Types of spring diving.
- What are three common types of spring diving?
- What are some considerations for each?

Spring diving equipment and planning.
- What types of diving equipment might you consider for your dive bag or dive box when spring diving?
- What are four safety considerations for spring diving?
- What are five things you should consider when planning a spring dive?

Knowledge Development Teaching Outline

A. Course Introduction

1. Staff and student diver introductions.

> **Note:**
>
> Introduce yourself and your assistants. Explain your background with spring diving if your student divers aren't familiar with you.
>
> Have divers introduce themselves and explain why they are interested in spring diving. Break the ice and encourage a relaxed atmosphere.
>
> Give times, dates and locations as appropriate for classroom presentations, confined water sessions, and open water dives.
>
> Review with students other skills they'll want as a PADI Spring Diver Distinctive Specialty Diver. These opportunities, through additional specialty course training, may include, but are not limited to: PADI Enriched Air Diver, PADI Deep Diver, PADI Peak Performance Buoyancy Diver, PADI Project AWARE Specialist, PADI Underwater Naturalist, PADI Underwater Videographer, PADI Digital Underwater Photographer, PADI Cavern Diver, PADI Drift Diver, and PADI Emergency Oxygen Provider.

2. Course Goals – this course will help students:
   a. Develop practical knowledge of spring diving environments, techniques, procedures, and considerations.
   b. Increase and improve diving skills.
   c. Plan, organize, and conduct spring dives.
   d. Improve diving ability by providing additional supervised expertise.
   e. Gain encouragement to participate in other PADI specialty training.

Spring Diver

3. Course Overview:
   a. **Knowledge development.** Confined water surface practice sessions are optional.
   b. **Open water dives. There will be at least two open water dives.** If possible, the dives should be in two different springs to provide variety, enhance students' comfort levels in a variety of environments, and improve their levels of diving experience.

4. Certification.
   a. Upon successfully completing the course, students will receive the PADI Spring Diver Distinctive Specialty certification.
   b. Certification means that students will be qualified to:
      1. Plan, organize, and make dives in conditions generally comparable to or better than those in which students were trained.
      2. Apply for the Master Scuba Diver rating if a student is a PADI Advanced Open Water Diver, a PADI Rescue Diver (or hold a qualifying certification from another training organization), is certified in four other PADI Specialty or Distinctive Specialty ratings, and has 50 logged dives.

> **Note:**
> Use the PADI Student Record File and/or PADI Continuing Education Administrative Document. Explain all course costs and materials, and what the costs do and do not include, including equipment use, dive site fees, etc. Explain what equipment student divers must have for the course, and what you will provide. Cover and review points about scheduling and attendance.

5. Class requirements.
   a. Complete all paperwork.
   b. Course costs.
   c. Equipment needs.
   d. Schedule and attendance.

Spring Diver — Instructor Guide

B. Why do people dive in springs? What are some advantages and disadvantages?

- ### What is spring diving?

Not all divers are fortunate enough to have easy access to the ocean, and most divers do not own their own boats. Spring diving can offer an easily accessible, local and often inexpensive way for divers to explore the underwater environment, train, practice skills, and enjoy diving without travel to the beach or the logistics of a journey to an exotic location.

Spring diving can be defined as scuba diving in any natural aquatic environment where fresh water flows from an *aquifer* to the earth's surface. Springs are a component of the *hydrosphere*, which is the combined mass of water found on, under, and above the earth.

- ### What are four advantages of spring diving?

Spring diving is associated with four advantages:

1. *Springs are often easily accessible by vehicle.* At many springs, divers can suit up directly out of their cars and walk straight to the entry point, or carry their gear only a short distance to a staging area. In these cases, dedicated surface support or supervision is not typically necessary.

2. *Spring diving is generally much less expensive* than boat diving in the ocean. Because of their natural beauty, many springs are either controlled by state or national park systems, or operated as private dive resorts. Either way, entry fees tend to be inexpensive compared to the cost of ocean diving on a commercial dive boat.

3. *Visibility tends to be superior* (often in excess of 100 feet) because freshwater springs are fed by underground aquifers. Spring water is typically filtered, clarified, and cleaned through the *water cycle*.

4. *Water temperature in springs tends to remain constant and predictable year-round* because of springs' unique position in the hydrosphere and water cycle.

- ### What are five concerns of spring diving?

Spring diving has five concerns that this course will teach you to address:

1. *Sections of some springs have overhead environments, or access to them.* Because freshwater springs are fed from underground aquifers, they sometimes have areas that are classified

Spring Diver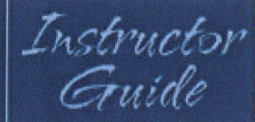

as *caverns* or *caves*. Both caverns and caves are called *overhead environments*, which means there is *no direct vertical access to the surface*. One of the most important safety factors in open water diving is that a diver who is low on air, out of air, separated from a buddy team, or has an equipment failure or other underwater emergency has direct vertical access to the surface. Being in an overhead environment removes this important safety contingency.

No divers in the Spring Diver course should enter an overhead environment unless they are properly equipped and Cavern or Cave Diver certified. To further discourage this, it is recommended that *only the PADI Spring Diver Distinctive Specialty Instructor should carry a light* on most open water spring dives, and only if permitted by local regulations. Many springs that feature cavern and cave sections do not allow non-cavern or non-cave certified divers to carry lights; this helps discourage them from straying into overhead environments.

2. *Some springs have very silty bottoms*. Bottom composition varies widely between different springs, as does the amount and speed of water inflow and outflow. Both these factors can affect the potential for "silting out" an area with as little as a careless fin kick. Students should be encouraged to remain off the bottom, practice good neutral buoyancy techniques, and use appropriate fin kicks for the environment. Flutter kicks, frog kicks, and bent-knee kicks are examples, and should be explained or demonstrated by the instructor.

3. *Dive etiquette and crowd control*. The advantages of spring diving tend to make it very popular in some areas, both for recreational diving and as dive training sites. However, unlike saltwater diving, freshwater springs by their nature have finite boundaries. A summer weekend might find a spring occupied at the same time by many types of divers ranging from snorkelers and beginning Open Water Diver classes to advanced tec divers, rebreathers and cave divers. Students should be encouraged to follow proper dive etiquette and to avoid creating or participating in "traffic jams" underwater or at entry/exit points.

4. *Outflow and inflow.* Because springs are connected to the aquifer, they can have strong outflow vents that should be considered in dive planning. A first or second magnitude spring can have *65 million gallons of outflow or more* into the spring *per day*. Depending on the size of the gap from which underground water flows into the spring, outflow can create enough water pressure to push divers backward as though they had just entered a strong current. Strong outflow can even knock off a mask if a diver is improperly positioned or does not have adequate situational awareness.

Less commonly, some springs have both outflow and *inflow* points. These inflow points are called *siphons*. Some larger siphons have noticeable suction inwards or downwards into a cave or tunnel system. Caution should be used around both outflow vents and inflow siphons. However, both vents and siphons tend to be directional and focused. As a result, the effects of a strong vent or siphon can often be mitigated simply by moving several feet to one side or the other of the outflow or intake. Encourage students to research a spring's features *before* they enter the water. It's very likely someone else has dove the spring before you – don't reinvent the wheel.

5. *Emergency and contingency planning.* Many spring dives are in areas where emergency assistance or equipment may not be immediately available, unlike on commercial dive boats that have other trained personnel onboard. In the case of an emergency or injury, you may be the most well-qualified person to manage the scene until EMS personal arrive.

- Always consider safety when planning your spring dives, especially in unsupervised or remote areas.
- Always have an Emergency Action Plan (EAP) for every spring you dive.
- Ensure you have a "save-a-dive" kit, a first aid kit, and emergency O2 with you as appropriate for the local spring environment.
- A good spring diver researches a spring before he or she dives it. Methods of research vary from asking questions of park rangers to searching social media and watching YouTube videos. Be creative in your research.
- Make sure someone ashore knows where, when and with whom you will be diving, and the anticipated time your group will be out of the water. Some spring diving sites (state parks in particular) require divers to leave their certification cards on the dashboards of their vehicles to help provide accountability at the end of the day.

C. Spring diving environments.

• What is a spring?

A *spring* is usually defined as natural aquatic environment where fresh water flows from an *aquifer* to the earth's surface. This happens when an aquifer either 1) intersects a natural or man-made depression on the surface; or 2) is filled or saturated to the point that water overflows onto the surface. Springs range in size from intermittent *seeps*, which flow only after heavy and persistent rain, to huge pools with outflows of over a hundred million gallons per day. The outflow from a seep can be barely detectable, while the outflow from a first-magnitude spring can be over *65 million gallons a day/100 cubic feet of water per second*.

Spring Diver — Instructor Guide

Springs are a component of the hydrosphere, which is the combined mass of water found on, under, and above the earth. Springs are part of the hydrosphere's *water cycle*. As rain, water is full of various impurities. When it falls and hits the earth's surface, it begins a filtering or "percolating" process through soil, and sometimes through different layers of rock called the *aquifer*. As it passes through these rock layers, it continues filtering. In time, the water can reach a body of water such as a spring and become surface water again. Because of this filtering process, by the time water reaches a spring it is often quite clear, pure and even drinkable.

Throughout history and throughout the world, people and animals have tended to live near springs because they need fresh water. However, in the modern day it is not a good idea in most cases to take out your regulator and have a long drink of cool, refreshing natural spring water from your dive site. The process of groundwater percolation through an aquifer usually filters debris and mud, and if water remains underground long enough the lack of sunlight causes most algae to die. However, many microbes and bacteria do not die just from being underground, and agricultural or industrial pollutants can remain in the water.

• How are springs formed?

In simple terms, the groundwater system associated with springs consists of three elements: a *recharge area* where water enters the subsurface; an *aquifer* or set of aquifers through which the water flows; and a *discharge point* where water emerges as a spring. A range of geological structures and topographic features can direct water to the surface and form a spring. Many seeps and small springs are associated with topographic depressions where the water table intersects the Earth's surface. Larger springs usually are formed where geological structures, such as rock faults and fractures, or layers of low-permeability material, force large amounts of water to the surface.

Springs are formed through the *water cycle* process.

1. Rainwater falls and collects on the surface of the earth. Unless it falls directly onto an existing body of water it either lands directly on, or eventually arrives at, a relatively thin layer of soil. Although some of the water evaporates directly, much of it can soak into the ground as *infiltration*.

2. Underneath the soil layer of the earth are layers of different types of rock or clay. Some rocks and clay are *impervious* to water, but in some areas the rock is in *permeable layers*. Examples of permeable rock layers are limestone, dolomite and sandstone.

3. Rainfall that seeps into the ground and/or permeable rock goes through a process called *percolation*. During this process, water travels downward through the tiny spaces between rocks and soil particles and into the absorbent permeable rock, much like water

fills and passes through the small holes of a sponge. The water eventually either <u>saturates</u> the underlying rock, in which case the "sponge" becomes full and overflows, or it <u>filters through</u> the permeable rock until it reaches a layer of impervious rock or clay and cannot continue in the same direction.

4. If the water reaches an impervious layer, it obeys the laws of gravity and follows the layer's contour, flowing downward or laterally along the underground surface. The saturated zone above the impervious layer is called the *water table*. Water continues to flow or seep along the impervious layer until it eventually intersects with a topographic depression at the surface of the earth. These intersections are where water tables and aquifers help fill springs, rivers, and lakes.

5. If the impervious layer is generally flat, water continues to soak into the sponge-like rock layer above it until the permeable layer is *saturated*. This saturation creates pressure that eventually drives water back to the surface, where it helps fill a spring, river or lake.

6. In either case, it is this process of infiltration, percolation, filtration and saturation that allows rainfall to ultimately replenish the water that flows from springs. Depending on the location and topography, the process can take anywhere from a few days to over a hundred years.

- ## What is an aquifer?

An *aquifer* is an underground layer of water-bearing permeable rock, rock fractures, or other porous material such as gravel or sand that filters groundwater after it passes through the soil layer. Water can move relatively easily through an aquifer's pores. The aquifer combines with surface and underground topography as part of the water cycle to eventually direct water back to the surface and create springs.

When depressions on the earth's surface intersect with an aquifer, they can become seeps or small springs with relatively low outflow. When impervious rock layers below the aquifer create pressure and direct large amounts of water back to the surface through rock faults or fractures, larger springs with greater outflow can form.

- **What is karst?**

    Karst is a unique underground terrain created when soluble rocks, principally limestone, dolomite and sandstone, begin to dissolve through the action of the water cycle. Karst areas are characterized by springs, caves, sinkholes, and create highly productive aquifers. Karst is created when water dissolves soluble rocks through the water cycle's process of percolation and saturation. These rocks erode over time, creating caves and other channels where water can move easily. On the surface, karst areas may feature deep fractures, caves, disappearing streams, springs, or sinkholes. Karst areas can be isolated, found in clusters, or cover large regions. They may be open, covered, buried, or partially filled with soil, rocks, plants, water or debris.

    Karst fields are found worldwide. About 20 percent of the land surface in the United States is classified as karst. Some of the largest karst areas in the U.S. are in Florida, Georgia, South Carolina, Kentucky, Missouri, Ohio and Wisconsin. Overseas, China, Europe and Australia are also known for large karst fields. Australia's vast Nullarbor Plain, on the borders of Western Australia and South Australia, is the world's largest karst field and covers over 200,000 square kilometres/77,000 square miles. Geologists, hydrologists and other researchers work to develop new ways of understanding and managing karst as a valuable, unique water-related resource.

- **Explain the different types and classifications of springs.**

    One way that springs are classified is by the volume of water they discharge. The largest springs are called "first magnitude," meaning they discharge on average at least 65 million gallons of water per day. In Florida, an area in the United States known for a large number and wide variety of springs, there are 33 first magnitude springs.

    The amount of water that flows from springs depends on many factors. These can include the size and composition of fissures or cracks within underground rocks; the water pressure in the aquifer; and the amount of rainfall. Human activities also can influence the volume of water that discharges from a spring. For example, excessive groundwater withdrawals in agricultural or populated areas can cause water levels in the aquifer to drop, which over time can decrease the flow from springs even many miles away.

Spring Diver — Instructor Guide

> ## Note:
> **Springs are classified by their average outflow, as follows:**
> - 1st Magnitude: Outflow is 100 cubic ft/sec or more, or 65 million gallons/day or more.
> - 2nd Magnitude: Outflow is 10-100 cubic ft/sec, or 6.5-65 million gallons/day.
> - 3rd Magnitude: Outflow is 1-10 cubic ft/sec, or .65-6.5 million gallons/day.
> - 4th-8th Magnitude: Outflow is less than 1 cubic ft/sec, or less than .65 million gallons/day.

- ## What are the general characteristics of springs?

Spring water can move through aquifers quickly, or very slowly. The "age" of spring water (the amount of time since it first hit the earth as rain and began percolating through to the aquifer) in any given spring can be anywhere from a few days to 100 years old. In general, when water age is "old," variations in the outflow of water from a spring are small. In contrast, springs with large variations in outflow have "younger" water.

Water from springs usually is remarkably clear. Water from some springs, however, may have color. For example, some natural springs in the western United States are reddish because of iron and minerals from ancient volcanic activity in the area. In Florida, some spring waters are described as "tea-colored" because they contain natural tannic acids from bark and other organic plant material picked up by groundwater during the percolation process. Tea-colored water in tannic springs can indicate that groundwater enters the aquifer near a spring, flows quickly through large channels inside the aquifer without fully percolating through porous rock, and outflows at a nearby spring vent. From a spring diver's perspective, tannic water is not hazardous to either health or scuba equipment. However, it can make for low visibility and necessitate carrying lights even in non-overhead environments.

Spring Diver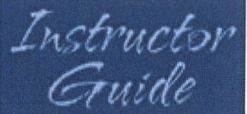

- ## What is a thermocline? What is a halocline? What are their relationships to spring diving?

1. Thermoclines.

According to PADI's *Encyclopedia of Recreational Diving*, a *thermocline* is a zone in which water temperature changes abruptly with depth. Thermoclines occur when differences in water temperature create differences in water density, which causes water to separate into layers. Relatively warm, low-density surface waters thereby create a distinct layer on top of colder, high-density, deeper waters. Thermoclines can be so abrupt that a diver can have part of his or her body in warmer water, and another part in distinctly colder water.

Thermoclines may or may not be a planning factor for spring divers. The temperature of spring water is directly related to the type and rate of spring outflow, as well as the average temperature and geography of the dive site. As depth increases below the earth's surface, it tends to have an insulating or even warming effect on groundwater. If spring outflow is low and a spring is small, most of the heat in the underground water will be conducted though rocks before it returns to the earth's surface as a spring, and a thermocline may occur. Even if outflow is greater, if a spring is large a thermocline may occur at depth. This is because the volume of water in the spring is too great to be adequately warmed. Students' pre-dive research should help reveal these and other characteristics of any given spring.

The warmest springs occur when discharges are at least moderately large, and often are found in regions where the subsurface is unusually warm or consistently warm year-round. In Florida, for example, springs with high outflow tend to remain at a constant 72-degree temperature throughout the year. This is because most rain in Florida falls during the warmer months and so its temperature is already relatively warm, as is the ground temperature. Florida's large karst layer has an additional insulating and heat-conserving effect on the groundwater as it percolates and moves through the aquifer, mixing with older warm water that is already in the aquifer. After being insulated or even warmed underground, the groundwater eventually vents as outflow to surface springs at a constant temperature – regardless of the ambient air temperature. In such hydrosystems, especially when spring water originates from deeper parts of the aquifer, thermoclines are generally only found in springs that have very low outflow. Many springs in Florida with significant outflow have no thermocline at all, because the water is always being rapidly renewed year-round with warm, consistent 72-degree water from the aquifer.

2.. Haloclines.

Just as temperature can create layers in water, so can water *type*. The *Encyclopedia of Recreational Diving* defines a halocline as a zone where the water type changes at depth due to an abrupt change in salinity, creating a distinct layer. This unique phenomenon is found in some springs near the ocean where fresh water from the aquifer mixes with salt water. Because the salt water is denser and heavier, the fresh water creates a layer over it. This is called a *salinity gradient*, which is a sharp boundary between a surface layer of fresh water and a layer of saltwater trapped below it. Fresh water is lighter than saltwater and can rise above it in a layer, forming a sharp salinity gradient called a *halocline*.

For a spring diver, a halocline can manifest as a cloudy, blurred or "halo" effect when crossing the layer or salinity gradient. If the layer is pronounced enough, it can even block out the sun – creating conditions very similar to night diving. Haloclines are much less common than thermoclines in spring diving, but represent a significant factor in spring dive planning and the decision whether or not to carry primary and backup lights. This is particularly important in springs with a significant halocline that can block natural light entirely, even in the middle of the day.

D. Types of spring diving.

- ### What are three common types of spring diving?

1. Shore spring diving.
2. Boat spring diving.
3. Drift spring diving.

- ### What are some considerations for each?

Shore spring diving – Divers generally can gear up directly from their vehicles, especially if the spring is located in a park or resort tailored to divers. If it is a long distance to the entry point, another option is to tote equipment by cart or dolly to a convenient staging location. Consider the overall physical fitness of your student divers when determining logistics. Dive flags are typically not required for most spring dives because there is no boat traffic in springs with finite shore boundaries; however, check local regulations.

Spring Diver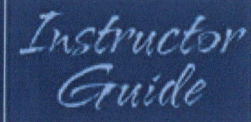

If the spring dive site is operated by a public or private entity there may be entry fees, waivers to sign and specific check-in/check-out procedures. Some springs inside U.S. state parks do not have a continuous presence inside the ranger station, and instead have only an "honor box" for small fees and a requirement for divers to place their certification cards on the dashboards of their vehicles for accountability. Be a good role model for other divers and follow all required procedures, even if the spring dive site is unsupervised by local officials.

Boat spring diving – Some springs, especially those bounded by private property and connected to a river system, are only accessible by boat. In this case, options for reaching the dive site can include commercial dive boat operators, pontoon boats, canoes or kayaks. If diving from small private watercraft, they either can be secured to shore or anchored to the bottom of the spring if appropriate and not environmentally sensitive or prohibited by local regulations. In addition, dive flags and floats should be used according to local regulations due to the potential for boat traffic in the area.

Drift spring diving – Some springs are part of, or connected to, a river system that is fed primarily by the spring's outflow. In this case, it may be possible to:
   a. Begin the dive <u>upriver</u> from the planned dive site;
   b. Drift dive or snorkel downriver to the dive site;
   c. Dive the intended spring;
   d. Continue drifting/snorkeling down the river to a predetermined exit point.

Another option might be to:
   a. Begin <u>downriver;</u>
   b. Take a boat upriver to the spring dive site;
   c. Drift back to a predetermined exit point when the spring dive is complete.

In both cases, dive floats and flags may be necessary or required; use them as appropriate. As always, be creative and thorough in your pre-dive planning and execution.

Spring Diver

> *Note:*
> Always consider safety when planning your dives, especially in unsupervised areas, and always have an Emergency Action Plan (EAP) for every spring you dive. Make sure someone ashore knows where, when and with whom you will be diving, and the anticipated time your group will be out of the water.
>
> In the case of an emergency, <u>you may be the most well-qualified person onsite to manage the event</u> until EMS personal arrive. Calmly take charge of the scene and enlist others for help as necessary.
>
> As with any dive:
> - Plan the dive and dive the plan.
> - Mentally rehearse potential problems and how you would deal with them.
> - Be alert for problems before, during and after the dive.
> - Try to anticipate and prevent problems BEFORE they happen.

E. Spring diving equipment and planning.

- **What types of diving equipment might you consider for your dive bag or dive box when spring diving?**
    - If gearing up from vehicles, a dive BOX or plastic tote is often much easier to transport and work from than a traditional dive bag that you would carry on a boat. Large totes or crates are inexpensive and available at hardware and many other retail stores.
    - Lines, reels, floats and flags as appropriate.
    - Knife/diver tool capable of cutting lines, especially if people are permitted to fish at or near the dive site.
    - First aid kit.
    - Emergency O2 kit and AED (if not readily available at dive site).

Spring Diver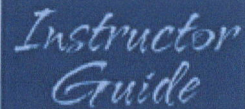

- "Save-a-dive" kit. The nearest dive shop may be miles away, and you often may be the most expert diver on the scene. Be prepared to handle any student equipment problems, and bring spares such as regulators and tanks. Encourage students to take the PADI *Equipment Specialist* course for continued education on how to handle common equipment problems.
- A tarp or mat on which to place equipment and suit up in unpaved areas. Your equipment will thank you, and it makes for a much cleaner pre-dive and post-dive.
- Primary and backup lights (if appropriate for local environment), typically for instructor use only. In general, students should be discouraged from carrying lights in the PADI *Spring Diver Distinctive Specialty* course if there is any chance of straying into an overhead environment. This helps encourage students to remain in natural light zones, and to not enter any overhead or cavern environments without direct vertical access to the surface.

• What are four safety considerations for spring diving?

1. Do not enter any overhead environments, caverns or caves unless properly trained, certified and equipped to do so.

2. Beware of strong outflow or inflow. Research a spring as much as possible before diving it.

3. Be self-sufficient both on the surface and underwater, and encourage students to be the same. This includes having an Emergency Action Plan, emergency O2 (if appropriate), a first aid kit, and extra equipment and spare parts.

4. Ensure neutral buoyancy and appropriate finning techniques to preserve the aquatic environment and prevent silting.

• What are five things you should consider when planning a spring dive?

1. Type of spring dive – shore, boat or drift? Plan and equip accordingly.

2. Logistics – gear up at vehicles, or use a wagon, cart, backpack, ATV or other means to carry equipment closer to the dive site?

Spring Diver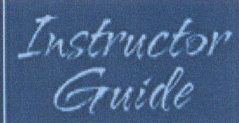

3. Contingency planning – what is the timeliness and availability of emergency medical services (EMS) and oxygen in case of emergency? How can EMS be reached? What communications are available if you need outside assistance of any type?

4. Streamline gear – some springs contain fallen trees or other potential entanglement hazards.

5. Certification level and capability of dive party members. Some springs are dark, tannic and deep, with bottoms well below the 130-foot limit of recreational diving. Always dive safely, conservatively, and within the limits of the divers in your group with the lowest levels of certification and competency.

Section Three: Open Water Dives

Confined Water Assessments or Training (Optional)

Conduct

There are no required confined water dives, surface practice sessions, or water skills assessments for the PADI Spring Diver Distinctive Specialty course. However, it is sound procedure to develop and/or assess student diver abilities in conditions that don't add complexity to learning new skills or new environments. For example, you may have students perform surface buoyancy checks in fresh water, neutral buoyancy skills, effective entries and exits, practice descents, maneuvering with a float, finning techniques, and other techniques applicable to spring diving before progressing to more challenging conditions. Entering the water quickly as a group through one or two openings marked on a dock or poolside can notably improve performance and dive etiquette in springs that may be crowded with divers, snorkelers, or even boaters.

You may add confined water or surface practice sessions at your discretion. The confined water session may also include a water skills assessment if a diver is unfamiliar to you. Emphasize that no matter what the level of certification or experience, divers should always mentally rehearse the dive and conduct thorough pre-dive planning, proper buddy procedures, descents, ascents, neutral buoyancy, environmentally sound finning techniques, and other spring diving skills.

Spring Diver

Open Water Dives

Conduct

On Dive One, students mainly acquaint themselves with the freshwater spring environment and practice common spring diving techniques like appropriate dive planning, entry, buoyancy checks, neutral buoyancy during the dive, no-silt finning, hovering, exiting and debriefing. The specifics of meeting those requirements may differ according to the type of spring environment you are diving in, and you may choose to demonstrate and practice additional techniques and procedures. Help students properly log the dive when it is complete.

It is encouraged to conduct open water dives in two or more different springs. Even if both dives are similar, it is recommended that you vary the techniques and procedures if possible and reasonable for the situation. For example, you may use a giant stride buoyant entry with a float for the first dive, but opt for a walk-in entry without a float for the second dive.

On Dive Two, students should continue developing and practicing Dive One skills. In addition, they should focus on the features and ecosystem specific to the spring they are diving. Are there fossils in the walls of the spring? How strong is the outflow and/or inflow? What magnitude is the spring? What aquatic plants, vertebrates and invertebrates can be identified? What is the bottom composition? These types of questions and observations should be addressed in both the pre-dive brief and the post-dive debriefing and dive logging.

> **Note:**
>
> If possible, it is recommended that you vary the spring diving environments and conduct the two required open water dives in two different springs. This helps broaden students' experience and exposes them to different logistics, techniques, and dive planning considerations.
>
> Although two successful open water spring dives in one location is the minimum for PADI Spring Diver Distinctive Specialty certification, you are encouraged to conduct additional dives at your discretion. An example might be: two dives in one spring on Day One, and two dives in a different spring on Day Two.
>
> In no case should more than three dives be conducted in one day. Bottom time on each dive should not exceed the no-decompression limits of the Recreational Dive Planner or each diver's computer.

Open Water Guidelines for Spring Dives

A. General Open Water Considerations

1. Involve student divers in as many pre-dive planning activities as possible. Have student divers research the spring dive site(s) and associated logistics, consider factors in Emergency Action Planning, determine types of equipment needed for the spring dives, and mentally rehearse.

2. Conduct the PADI Spring Diver Distinctive Specialty course in at least two different springs if possible.

3. Conduct a thorough briefing. The better the briefing, the more smoothly the spring dives will proceed. In addition to discussing dive profiles, conditions and facilities at the dive site, pre-dive briefings should consider entry and exit techniques, spring topography and hydrography, use or non-use of lights, no-silt finning and neutral buoyancy techniques, how the group will stay together, planned and unplanned stops, types of geologic features and aquatic life to expect, bottom composition, the importance of avoiding overhead environments/caverns/caves, and when the group will ascend.

Spring Diver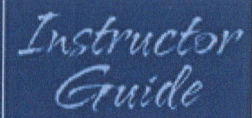

4. Spring diving is generally not complicated, but as with any dive, detailed planning is required to ensure the group dives in a coordinated and safe manner. Do a roll call before entering the water, regardless of whether your group is large or small. Review all emergency protocols with both students and assistants. Evaluate divers' thermal protection and ensure it is appropriate for the dive site and expected conditions. Be available to answer questions or provide guidance during equipment assembly, safety checks and gearing up.

5. The use of certified assistants is highly recommended. Assistants can help keep the group together and accounted for, while allowing you to focus on individual performances and anticipating potential problems before they happen.

6. **Regardless of how you conduct the open water dives, student divers must demonstrate the following performance requirements to qualify for certification:**

Spring Diver - Open Water Dive One

By the end of Open Water Dive One, students will be able to:

- Within the overall group and with a buddy, plan a spring dive accounting for logistics, techniques and equipment for the appropriate environment, conditions, depth, and other variables.
- Demonstrate an entry specific to the environmental conditions of the spring and the planned dive.
- Conduct a buoyancy check at the surface as appropriate, and ensure proper weighting for neutral buoyancy.
- Make a controlled, slow descent to a predetermined depth without touching the bottom of the spring. If needed, adjust for neutral buoyancy using the BCD.
- Demonstrate appropriate buoyancy control and other techniques throughout the spring dive, including neutral buoyancy, streamlining, appropriate finning, and avoiding accidental or damaging contact with the environment.
- Hover for 30 seconds without rising or sinking more than 1 metre/3 feet by making minor depth adjustments using breath control or BCD.
- Demonstrate efficient fin kicks and no-silt finning techniques throughout the spring dive.
- If possible in the selected spring environment and depth, travel at least 8 metres/25 feet while swimming horizontally no more than 1 metre/3 feet above the spring bottom, without silting the surrounding area or touching any aquatic plants.
- Do NOT enter ANY overhead environment without direct vertical access to the surface, including underwater shelfs, ledges, caverns or caves, unless properly trained and certified.
- Demonstrate an exit from the water specific to the spring dive site and environmental conditions.

Spring Diver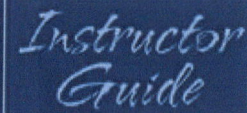

Spring Diver - Open Water Dive Two

By the end of Open Water Dive Two, students will be able to:

- Within the overall group and with a buddy, plan a spring dive accounting for logistics, techniques and equipment for the appropriate environment, conditions, depth, and other variables.
- Demonstrate an entry specific to the environmental conditions of the spring and the planned dive.
- Make a controlled, slow descent to a predetermined depth without touching the bottom of the spring. If needed, adjust for neutral buoyancy using the BCD.
- Demonstrate appropriate buoyancy control, finning and other techniques throughout the spring dive, and continue honing Dive One skills.
- Use pre-dive site research to look for and identify features of the spring and elements of its unique ecosystem while diving. Examples may include:
    - Are there fossils in the spring walls? What are they?
    - Identify location(s) and estimate strength of inflow and/or outflow from spring vent(s) and/or siphon(s).
    - Magnitude of spring and bottom composition.
    - What aquatic plants, vertebrates and invertebrates can be identified?
    - Other features unique to the spring.
- Do NOT enter ANY overhead environment without direct vertical access to the surface, including underwater shelves, ledges, caverns or caves, unless properly trained and certified.
- Demonstrate an exit from the water specific to the spring dive site and environmental conditions.

B. Open Water Dives for Spring Diver

Dive One

- Within the overall group and with a buddy, plan a spring dive accounting for logistics, techniques and equipment for the appropriate environment, conditions, depth, and other variables.
- Demonstrate an entry specific to the environmental conditions of the spring and the planned dive.
- Conduct a buoyancy check at the surface as appropriate, and ensure proper weighting for neutral buoyancy.
- Make a controlled, slow descent to to a predetermined depth without touching the bottom of the spring. If needed, adjust for neutral buoyancy using the BCD.
- Demonstrate appropriate buoyancy control and other techniques throughout the spring dive, including neutral buoyancy, streamlining, appropriate finning, and avoiding accidental or damaging contact with the environment.
- Hover for 30 seconds without rising or sinking more than 1 metre/3 feet by making minor depth adjustments using breath control or BCD.
- Demonstrate efficient fin kicks and no-silt finning techniques throughout the spring dive.
- If possible in the selected spring environment and depth, travel at least 8 metres/25 feet while swimming horizontally no more than 1 metre/3 feet above the spring bottom, without silting the surrounding area or touching any aquatic plants.
- Do NOT enter ANY overhead environment without direct vertical access to the surface, including underwater shelfs, ledges, caverns or caves, unless properly trained and certified.
- Demonstrate an exit from the water specific to the spring dive site and environmental conditions.

1. Briefing
   a. Review and discuss pre-dive planning for the specific spring
   b. Facilities at dive site
   c. Entry/exit techniques to be used
   d. Bottom composition and topography/hydrography of dive site
   e. Depth range on bottom
   f. Ending tank pressure – when to terminate the dive
   g. Interesting and helpful facts about the dive site, do not touch sensitive artifacts like fossils

Spring Diver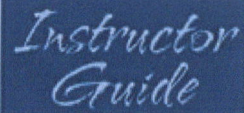

2. **Dive Sequence – restate Dive One required tasks**
   a. Assemble gear and suit up
   b. Predive safety check – BWRAF
   c. Enter water using appropriate technique
   d. Buoyancy check at the surface
   e. Maintain buddy contact and awareness
   f. Neutral buoyancy, hovering, streamlining and finning techniques
   g. Avoid contact with the bottom – goal is no silt
   h. No diver will enter an overhead environment unless planned, properly certified, and properly equipped.
   i. Dive for fun and pleasure
   j. Ascend with 3-minute safety stop
   k. Appropriate exit
   l. Post-dive debrief and log dive (instructor signs log)

Dive Two

- Within the overall group and with a buddy, plan a spring dive accounting for logistics, techniques and equipment for the appropriate environment, conditions, depth, and other variables.
- Demonstrate an entry specific to the environmental conditions of the spring and the planned dive.
- Make a controlled, slow descent to a predetermined depth without touching the bottom of the spring. If needed, adjust for neutral buoyancy using the BCD.
- Demonstrate appropriate buoyancy control, finning and other techniques throughout the spring dive, and continue honing Dive One skills.
- Use pre-dive site research or discussion to look for and identify features of the spring and elements of its unique ecosystem while diving. Examples may include:
- Are there fossils in the spring walls? What are they?
- Identify location(s) and estimate strength of inflow and/or outflow from spring vent(s) and/or siphon(s).
- Magnitude of spring and bottom composition.
- What aquatic plants, vertebrates and invertebrates can be identified?
- Other features unique to the spring.
- Do NOT enter ANY overhead environment without direct vertical access to the surface, including underwater shelves, ledges, caverns or caves, unless properly trained and certified.

Spring Diver — Instructor Guide

- **Demonstrate an exit from the water specific to the spring dive site and environmental conditions.**

1. Briefing
    a. Review and discuss pre-dive planning for the specific spring
    b. Facilities at dive site
    c. Entry/exit techniques to be used
    d. Bottom composition and topography/hydrography of dive site
    e. Depth range on bottom
    f. Ending tank pressure – when to terminate the dive
    g. Interesting and helpful facts about the dive site, do not touch sensitive artifacts like fossils

2. **Dive Sequence – restate Dive Two required tasks**
    a. Assemble gear and suit up
    b. Predive safety check – BWRAF
    c. Enter water using appropriate technique
    d. Buoyancy check at the surface
    e. Maintain buddy contact and awareness
    f. Neutral buoyancy, hovering, streamlining and finning techniques
    g. Use pre-dive research or discussion to look for and identify features of the spring and elements of its unique ecosystem while diving
    h. Avoid contact with the bottom – goal is no silt
    i. No diver will enter an overhead environment unless planned, properly certified, and properly equipped
    j. Dive for fun and pleasure
    k. Ascend with 3-minute safety stop
    l. Appropriate exit
    m. Post-dive debrief and log dive (instructor signs log)

Spring Diver

Post-Dive Debriefing Reminders:

- Encourage student divers to discuss their spring dive entry; descent; how they were able to control their buoyancy; their methods for maintaining buddy contact; awareness and avoidance of overhead environments; ascent and safety stop, and exit used.
- Guide the discussion to address what worked, what didn't work, and how things may be done differently next time. Discuss any possible hazards, problems, and solutions in detail. Discuss the procedures they planned to use in case of separation from the group. Talk about the aquatic life and interesting scenery seen on your dive.
- Guide the discussion to address what you and your staff observed working or not working. Make a point of correcting environmentally unfriendly behaviors, if observed.
- Emphasize the importance of logging dives. In particular, log the location, depth, bottom time, type of exposure suit, and amount of weight worn.
- Sign logbooks and explain that many spring dive sites, especially parks and resorts, have logbook stamps or stickers that most divers enjoy collecting.

Spring Diver

Appendix

Table of Contents

Spring Diver Knowledge Review Student Handout 38
Spring Diver Quick Review Answer Sheet... 50
Spring Diver Quick Review Answer Key.. 53
Specialty Training Record for Spring Diver... 56

Student Handout – Spring Diver

A. Why do people dive in springs? What are some advantages and disadvantages?

- **What is spring diving?**

    Not all divers are fortunate enough to have easy access to the ocean, and most divers do not own their own boats. Spring diving can offer an easily accessible, local and often inexpensive way for divers to explore the underwater environment, train, practice skills, and enjoy diving without travel to the beach or the logistics of a journey to an exotic location.

    Spring diving can be defined as scuba diving in any natural aquatic environment where fresh water flows from an *aquifer* to the earth's surface. Springs are a component of the *hydrosphere*, which is the combined mass of water found on, under, and above the earth.

- **What are four advantages of spring diving?**

Spring diving is associated with four advantages:

1. *Springs are often easily accessible by vehicle.* At many springs, divers can suit up directly out of their cars and walk straight to the entry point, or carry their gear only a short distance to a staging area. In these cases, dedicated surface support or supervision is not typically necessary.

2. *Spring diving is generally much less expensive* than boat diving in the ocean. Because of their natural beauty, many springs are either controlled by state or national park systems, or operated as private dive resorts. Either way, entry fees tend to be inexpensive compared to the cost of ocean diving on a commercial dive boat.

3. *Visibility tends to be superior* (often in excess of 100 feet) because freshwater springs are fed by underground aquifers. Spring water is typically filtered, clarified, and cleaned through the *water cycle*.

Spring Diver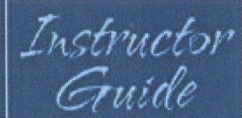

4. *Water temperature in springs tends to remain constant and predictable year-round* because of springs' unique position in the hydrosphere and water cycle.

• What are five concerns of spring diving?

Spring diving has five concerns that this course will teach you to address:

1. *Sections of some springs have overhead environments, or access to them.* Because freshwater springs are fed from underground aquifers, they sometimes have areas that are classified as *caverns* or *caves*. Both caverns and caves are called *overhead environments*, which means there is *no direct vertical access to the surface*. One of the most important safety factors in open water diving is that a diver who is low on air, out of air, separated from a buddy team, or has an equipment failure or other underwater emergency has direct vertical access to the surface. Being in an overhead environment removes this important safety contingency.

No divers in the Spring Diver course should enter an overhead environment unless they are properly equipped and Cavern or Cave Diver certified. To further discourage this, it is recommended that *only the PADI Spring Diver Distinctive Specialty Instructor should carry a light* on most open water spring dives, and only if permitted by local regulations. Many springs that feature cavern and cave sections do not allow non-cavern or non-cave certified divers to carry lights; this helps discourage them from straying into overhead environments.

2. *Some springs have very silty bottoms.* Bottom composition varies widely between different springs, as does the amount and speed of water inflow and outflow. Both these factors can affect the potential for "silting out" an area with as little as a careless fin kick. Good spring divers remain off the bottom, practice good neutral buoyancy techniques, and use appropriate fin kicks for the environment. Flutter kicks, frog kicks, and bent-knee kicks are examples.

3. *Dive etiquette and crowd control.* The advantages of spring diving tend to make it very popular in some areas, both for recreational diving and as dive training sites. However, unlike saltwater diving, freshwater springs by their nature have finite boundaries. A summer weekend might find a spring occupied at the same time by many types of divers ranging from snorkelers and beginning Open Water Diver classes to advanced tec divers, rebreathers and cave divers. Follow good dive etiquette and avoid creating or participating in "traffic jams" underwater or at entry/exit points.

Spring Diver

4. *Outflow and inflow.* Because springs are connected to the aquifer, they can have strong outflow vents that should be considered in dive planning. A first or second magnitude spring can have *65 million gallons of outflow or more* into the spring *per day*. Depending on the size of the gap from which underground water flows into the spring, outflow can create enough water pressure to push divers backward as though they had just entered a strong current. Strong outflow can even knock off a mask if a diver is improperly positioned or does not have adequate situational awareness. Less commonly, some springs have both outflow and *inflow* points. These inflow points are called *siphons*. Some larger siphons have noticeable suction inwards or downwards into a cave or tunnel system.

Caution should be used around both outflow vents and inflow siphons. However, both vents and siphons tend to be directional and focused. As a result, the effects of a strong vent or siphon can often be mitigated simply by moving several feet to one side or the other of the outflow or intake. Encourage students to research a spring's features *before* they enter the water. It's very likely someone else has dove the spring before you – don't reinvent the wheel.

5. *Emergency and contingency planning.* Many spring dives are in areas where emergency assistance or equipment may not be immediately available, unlike on commercial dive boats that have other trained personnel onboard. In the case of an emergency or injury, you may be the most well-qualified person to manage the scene until EMS personal arrive.
- Always consider safety when planning your spring dives, especially in unsupervised or remote areas.
- Always have an Emergency Action Plan (EAP) for every spring you dive.
- Ensure you have a "save-a-dive" kit, a first aid kit, and emergency O2 with you as appropriate for the local spring environment.
- A good spring diver researches a spring before he or she dives it. Methods of research vary from asking questions of park rangers to searching social media and watching YouTube videos. Be creative in your research.
- Make sure someone ashore knows where, when and with whom you will be diving, and the anticipated time your group will be out of the water. Some spring diving sites (state parks in particular) require divers to leave their certification cards on the dashboards of their vehicles to help provide accountability at the end of the day.

B. Spring diving environments.

- ### What is a spring?

A *spring* is usually defined as natural aquatic environment where fresh water flows from an *aquifer* to the earth's surface. This happens when an aquifer either 1) intersects a natural or man-made depression on the surface, or 2) is filled or saturated to the point that water overflows onto the surface. Springs range in size from intermittent *seeps*, which flow only after heavy and persistent rain, to huge pools with outflows of over a hundred million gallons per day. The outflow from a seep can be barely detectable, while the outflow from a first-magnitude spring can be over *65 million gallons a day/100 cubic feet of water per second*.

Springs are a component of the hydrosphere, which is the combined mass of water found on, under, and above the earth. Springs are part of the hydrosphere's *water cycle*. As rain, water is full of various impurities. When it falls and hits the earth's surface, it begins a filtering or "percolating" process through soil, and sometimes through different layers of rock called the *aquifer*. As it passes through these rock layers, it continues filtering. In time, the water can reach a body of water such as a spring and become surface water again. Because of this filtering process, by the time water reaches a spring it is often quite clear, pure and even drinkable.

Throughout history and throughout the world, people and animals have tended to live near springs because they need fresh water. However, in the modern day it is not a good idea in most cases to take out your regulator and have a long drink of cool, refreshing natural spring water from your dive site. The process of groundwater percolation through an aquifer usually filters debris and mud, and if water remains underground long enough the lack of sunlight causes most algae to die. However, many microbes and bacteria do not die just from being underground, and agricultural or industrial pollutants can remain in the water.

- ### How are springs formed?

In simple terms, the groundwater system associated with springs consists of three elements: a *recharge area* where water enters the subsurface; an *aquifer* or set of aquifers through which the water flows; and a *discharge point* where water emerges as a spring. A range of geological structures and topographic features can direct water to the surface and form a spring. Many seeps and small springs are associated with topographic depressions where the water table intersects the Earth's surface. Larger springs usually are formed where geological structures, such as rock faults and fractures, or layers of low-permeability material, force large amounts of water to the surface.

Springs are formed through the *water cycle* process:.

1. Rainwater falls and collects on the surface of the earth. Unless it falls directly onto an existing body of water it either lands directly on, or eventually arrives at, a relatively thin layer of soil. Although some of the water evaporates directly, much of it can soak into the ground as *infiltration*.

2. Underneath the soil layer of the earth are layers of different types of rock or clay. Some rocks and clay are *impervious* to water, but in some areas the rock is in *permeable layers*. Examples of permeable rock layers are limestone, dolomite and sandstone.

3. Rainfall that seeps into the ground and/or permeable rock goes through a process called *percolation*. During this process, water travels downward through the tiny spaces between rocks and soil particles and into the absorbent permeable rock, much as water fills and passes through the small holes of a sponge. The water eventually either <u>saturates</u> the underlying rock, in which case the "sponge" becomes full and overflows, or it <u>filters through</u> the permeable rock until it reaches a layer of impervious rock or clay and cannot continue in the same direction.

4. If the water reaches an impervious layer, it obeys the laws of gravity and follows the layer's contour, flowing downward or laterally along the underground surface. The saturated zone above the impervious layer is called the *water table*. Water continues to flow or seep along the impervious layer until it eventually intersects with a topographic depression at the surface of the earth. These intersections are where water tables and aquifers help fill springs, rivers, and lakes.

5. If the impervious layer is generally flat, water continues to soak into the sponge-like rock layer above it until the permeable layer is *saturated*. This saturation creates pressure that eventually drives water back to the surface, where it helps fill a spring, river, or lake.

6. In either case, it is this process of infiltration, percolation, filtration and saturation that allows rainfall to ultimately replenish the water that flows from springs. Depending on the location and topography, the process can take anywhere from a few days to over a hundred years.

- ## What is an aquifer?

An *aquifer* is an underground layer of water-bearing permeable rock, rock fractures, or other porous material such as gravel or sand that filters groundwater after it passes through the soil layer. Water can move relatively easily through an aquifer's pores. The aquifer combines with surface and underground topography as part of the water cycle to eventually direct water back to the surface and create springs.

When depressions on the earth's surface intersect with an aquifer, they can become seeps or small springs with relatively low outflow. When impervious rock layers below the aquifer create pressure and direct large amounts of water back to the surface through rock faults or fractures, larger springs with greater outflow can form.

- ## What is karst?

Karst is a unique underground terrain created when soluble rocks, principally limestone, dolomite and sandstone, begin to dissolve through the action of the water cycle. Karst areas are characterized by springs, caves, sinkholes, and create highly productive aquifers. Karst is created when water dissolves soluble rocks through the water cycle's process of percolation and saturation. These rocks erode over time, creating caves and other channels where water can move easily. On the surface, karst areas may feature deep fractures, caves, disappearing streams, springs, or sinkholes. Karst areas can be isolated, found in clusters, or cover large regions. They may be open, covered, buried, or partially filled with soil, rocks, plants, water or debris.

Karst fields are found worldwide. About 20 percent of the land surface in the United States is classified as karst. Some of the largest karst areas in the U.S. are in Florida, Georgia, South Carolina, Kentucky, Missouri, Ohio and Wisconsin. Overseas, China, Europe and Australia are also known for large karst fields. Australia's vast Nullarbor Plain, on the borders of Western Australia and South Australia, is the world's largest karst field and covers over 200,000 square kilometres/77,000 square miles. Geologists, hydrologists and other researchers work to develop new ways of understanding and managing karst as a valuable, unique water-related resource.

Spring Diver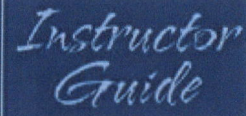

- ## Explain the different types and classifications of springs.

One way that springs are classified is by the volume of water they discharge. The largest springs are called "first magnitude," meaning they discharge on average at least 65 million gallons of water per day. In Florida, an area in the United States known for a large number and wide variety of springs, there are 33 first magnitude springs.

The amount of water that flows from springs depends on many factors. These can include the size and composition of fissures or cracks within underground rocks; the water pressure in the aquifer; and the amount of rainfall. Human activities also can influence the volume of water that discharges from a spring. For example, excessive groundwater withdrawals in agricultural or populated areas can cause water levels in the aquifer to drop, which over time can decrease the flow from springs even many miles away.

Note:

Springs are classified by their average outflow, as follows:

- 1st Magnitude: Outflow is 100 cubic ft/sec or more, or 65 million gallons/day or more.
- 2nd Magnitude: Outflow is 10-100 cubic ft/sec, or 6.5-65 million gallons/day.
- 3rd Magnitude: Outflow is 1-10 cubic ft/sec, or .65-6.5 million gallons/day.
- 4th-8th Magnitude: Outflow is less than 1 cubic ft/sec, or less than .65 million gallons/day.

- ## What are the general characteristics of springs?

Spring water can move through aquifers quickly, or very slowly. The "age" of spring water (the amount of time since it first hit the earth as rain and began percolating through to the aquifer) in any given spring can be anywhere from a few days to 100 years old. In general, when water age is "old," variations in the outflow of water from a spring are small. In contrast, springs with large variations in outflow have "younger" water.

Water from springs usually is remarkably clear. Water from some springs, however, may have color. For example, some natural springs in the western United States are reddish because of iron and minerals from ancient volcanic activity in the area. In Florida, some spring waters are described as "tea-colored" because they contain natural tannic acids from bark and other organic plant material picked up by groundwater during the percolation process. Tea-colored water in tannic springs can indicate that groundwater enters the aquifer near a spring, flows quickly through large channels inside the aquifer without fully percolating through porous rock, and outflows at a nearby spring vent. From a spring diver's perspective, tannic water is not hazardous to either health or scuba equipment. However, it can make for low visibility and necessitate carrying lights even in non-overhead environments.

- **What is a thermocline? What is a halocline? What are their relationships to spring diving?**

1. Thermoclines.

According to PADI's *Encyclopedia of Recreational Diving*, a *thermocline* is a zone in which water temperature changes abruptly with depth. Thermoclines occur when differences in water temperature create differences in water density, which causes water to separate into layers. Relatively warm, low-density surface waters thereby create a distinct layer on top of colder, high-density, deeper waters. Thermoclines can be so abrupt that a diver can have part of his or her body in warmer water, and another part in distinctly colder water.

Thermoclines may or may not be a planning factor for spring divers. The temperature of spring water is directly related to the type and rate of spring outflow, as well as the average temperature and geography of the dive site. As depth increases below the earth's surface, it tends to have an insulating or even warming effect on groundwater. If spring outflow is low and a spring is small, most of the heat in the underground water will be conducted though rocks before it returns to the earth's surface as a spring, and a thermocline may occur. Even if outflow is greater, if a spring is large a thermocline may occur at depth. This is because the volume of water in the spring is too great to be adequately warmed. Your pre-dive research should help reveal these and other characteristics of any given spring.

The warmest springs occur when discharges are at least moderately large, and often are found in regions where the subsurface is unusually warm or consistently warm year-round. In Florida, for example, springs with high outflow tend to remain at a constant 72-degree temperature throughout the year. This is because most rain in Florida falls during the warmer months and so its temperature is already relatively warm, as is the ground temperature. Florida's large karst layer has an additional insulating and heat-conserving effect on the groundwater as it percolates and moves through the aquifer, mixing with older warm water that is already in the aquifer. After being insulated or even warmed underground, the groundwater eventually vents as outflow to surface springs at a constant temperature – regardless of the ambient air temperature. In such hydrosystems, especially when spring water originates from deeper parts of the aquifer, thermoclines are generally only found in springs that have very low outflow. Many springs in Florida with significant outflow have no thermocline at all, because the water is always being rapidly renewed year-round with warm, consistent 72-degree water from the aquifer.

Spring Diver — Instructor Guide

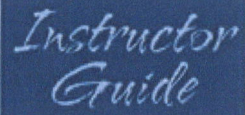

2. Haloclines.

   a. Just as temperature can create layers in water, so can water *type*. The *Encyclopedia of Recreational Diving* defines a halocline as a zone where the water type changes at depth due to an abrupt change in salinity, creating a distinct layer. This unique phenomenon is found in some springs near the ocean where fresh water from the aquifer mixes with salt water. Because the salt water is denser and heavier, the fresh water creates a layer over it. This is called a *salinity gradient*, which is a sharp boundary between a surface layer of fresh water and a layer of saltwater trapped below it. Fresh water is lighter than saltwater and can rise above it in a layer, forming a sharp salinity gradient called a *halocline*.

   For a spring diver, a halocline can manifest as a cloudy, blurred or "halo" effect when crossing the layer or salinity gradient. If the layer is pronounced enough, it can even block out the sun – creating conditions very similar to night diving. Haloclines are much less common than thermoclines in spring diving, but represent a significant factor in spring dive planning and the decision whether or not to carry primary and backup lights. This is particularly important in springs with a significant halocline that can block natural light entirely, even in the middle of the day.

C. Types of spring diving.

- **What are three common types of spring diving?**

1. Shore spring diving.
2. Boat spring diving.
3. Drift spring diving.

- **What are some considerations for each?**

Shore spring diving – Divers generally can gear up directly from their vehicles, especially if the spring is located in a park or resort tailored to divers. If it is a long distance to the entry point, another option is to tote equipment by cart or dolly to a convenient staging location. Consider the overall physical fitness of your dive party members when determining logistics. Dive flags are typically not required for most spring dives because there is no boat traffic in springs with finite shore boundaries; however, check local regulations.

Spring Diver

If the spring dive site is operated by a public or private entity there may be entry fees, waivers to sign and specific check-in/check-out procedures. Some springs inside U.S. state parks do not have a continuous presence inside the ranger station, and instead have only an "honor box" for small fees and a requirement for divers to place their certification cards on the dashboards of their vehicles for accountability. Be a responsible diver and follow all required procedures, even if the spring dive site is unsupervised by local officials.

Boat spring diving – Some springs, especially those bounded by private property and connected to a river system, are only accessible by boat. In this case, options for reaching the dive site can include commercial dive boat operators, pontoon boats, canoes or kayaks. If diving from small private watercraft, they either can be secured to shore or anchored to the bottom of the spring if appropriate and not environmentally sensitive or prohibited by local regulations. In addition, dive flags and floats should be used according to local regulations due to the potential for boat traffic in the area.

Drift spring diving – Some springs are part of, or connected to, a river system that is fed primarily by the spring's outflow. In this case, it may be possible to:
    a. Begin the dive <u>upriver</u> from the planned dive site;
    b. Drift dive or snorkel downriver to the dive site;
    c. Dive the intended spring;
    d. Continue drifting/snorkeling down the river to a predetermined exit point.

Another option might be to:
    a. Begin <u>downriver;</u>
    b. Take a boat upriver to the spring dive site;
    c. Drift back to a predetermined exit point when the spring dive is complete.

In both cases, dive floats and flags may be necessary or required; use them as appropriate. As always, be creative and thorough in your pre-dive planning and execution.

Spring Diver

D. Spring diving equipment and planning.

- **What types of diving equipment might you consider for your dive bag or dive box when spring diving?**
    - If gearing up from vehicles, a dive BOX or plastic tote is often much easier to transport and work from than a traditional dive bag that you would carry on a boat. Large totes or crates are inexpensive and available at hardware and many other retail stores.
    - Lines, reels, floats and flags as appropriate.
    - Knife/diver tool capable of cutting lines, especially if people are permitted to fish at or near the dive site.
    - First aid kit.
    - Emergency O2 kit and AED (if not readily available at dive site).
    - "Save-a-dive" kit. The nearest dive shop may be miles away, and you often may be the most expert diver on the scene. Be prepared to handle any student equipment problems, and bring spares such as regulators and tanks. Encourage students to take the PADI *Equipment Specialist* course for continued education on how to handle common equipment problems.
    - A tarp or mat on which to place equipment and suit up in unpaved areas. Your equipment will thank you, and it makes for a much cleaner pre-dive and post-dive.
    - Primary and backup lights (if appropriate for local environment), typically for instructor use only. In general, students should be discouraged from carrying lights in the PADI *Spring Diver Distinctive Specialty* course if there is any chance of straying into an overhead environment. This helps encourage students to remain in natural light zones, and to not enter any overhead or cavern environments without direct vertical access to the surface.

- **What are four safety considerations for spring diving?**

1. Do not enter any overhead environments, caverns or caves unless properly trained, certified and equipped to do so.

2. Beware of strong outflow or inflow. Research a spring as much as possible before diving it.

3. Be self-sufficient both on the surface and underwater, and encourage students to be the same. This includes having an Emergency Action Plan, emergency O2 (if appropriate), a first aid kit, and extra equipment and spare parts.

4. Ensure neutral buoyancy and appropriate finning techniques to preserve the aquatic environment and prevent silting.

- **What are five things you should consider when planning a spring dive?**

1. Type of spring dive – shore, boat or drift? Plan and equip accordingly.

2. Logistics – gear up at vehicles, or use a wagon, cart, backpack, ATV or other means to carry equipment closer to the dive site?

3. Contingency planning – what is the timeliness and availability of emergency medical services (EMS) and oxygen in case of emergency? How can EMS be reached? What communications are available if you need outside assistance of any type?

4. Streamline gear – some springs contain fallen trees or other potential entanglement hazards.

5. Certification level and capability of dive party members. Some springs are dark, tannic and deep, with bottoms well below the 130-foot limit of recreational diving. Always dive safely, conservatively, and within the limits of the divers in your group with the lowest levels of certification and competency.

Quick Review – Spring Diver

(Check all that apply)

1. **What is spring diving?**

   ☐ Diving during the spring equinox, also known as the vernal equinox.
   ☐ Scuba diving in any natural aquatic environment where fresh water flows from an aquifer to the earth's surface.
   ☐ A water-entry technique where a diver bounces off the platform like a spring.
   ☐ Diving in pool-like conditions.

2. **What is not an advantage of spring diving?**

   ☐ Springs are often easily accessible by vehicle.
   ☐ Spring diving is generally much less expensive than saltwater boat diving.
   ☐ There are many aquatic creatures in springs that can attack or hurt you.
   ☐ Visibility tends to be superior.

3. **What are some concerns of spring diving?**

   ☐ Sections of some springs have overhead environments or access to them.
   ☐ The amount of outflow and inflow through vents and siphons.
   ☐ Dive etiquette and crowd control.
   ☐ Some springs have very silty bottoms.

4. **What are three broad elements of the groundwater system associated with springs?**

   ☐ A recharge area or areas.
   ☐ One or more discharge points.
   ☐ An aquifer.
   ☐ Tidal flow caused by the lunar cycle.

Spring Diver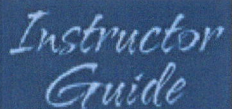

Quick Review – Spring Diver

(Check all that apply)

5. What is karst?

- [ ] A unique type of underground terrain created when soluble rocks such as limestone, dolomite and sandstone can filter or channel water.
- [ ] An aquatic grass often found in Australian springs.
- [ ] A type of specialized cave diving equipment.
- [ ] An impervious layer of rock or clay beneath the earth's surface.

6. What is the average outflow of a 1st magnitude spring?

- [ ] 100 cubic ft/sec or 65 million gallons/day, or more.
- [ ] 75 cubic ft/sec or 45 million gallons/day.
- [ ] No more than 100 cubic ft/sec or 65 million gallons/day.
- [ ] The answer cannot be determined from the information given.

7. What factors can affect the amount of water that discharges from springs?

- [ ] The size and composition of fissures within underground rocks.
- [ ] The water pressure in the aquifer.
- [ ] The amount of rainfall.
- [ ] Groundwater withdrawals from agricultural or populated areas far away.

8. You can't find your buddy in a dark and silty spring. What should you do?

- [ ] Turn on your light and use it to look for your buddy.
- [ ] Begin a circular search pattern, making sure to stay off the bottom.
- [ ] Swim into the overhead environment and see if your buddy went there.
- [ ] Follow standard safe diving procedures. Look for your buddy for no longer than one minute, then conduct a safe ascent and rejoin at the surface.

Quick Review – Spring Diver

(Check all that apply)

9. What is a halocline?

- [ ] A distinct layer in some springs where saltwater sits on top of fresh water.
- [ ] A zone where a saltwater layer is trapped below a freshwater layer.
- [ ] A unique feature of some springs near the ocean that can block sunlight.
- [ ] A temperature gradient in water where it changes from warm to cold.

10. What are the three types of spring diving?

- [ ] Drift spring diving.
- [ ] Shore spring diving.
- [ ] Thermal spring diving.
- [ ] Boat spring diving.

11. What things should a good spring diver have?

- [ ] Good buoyancy control.
- [ ] No-silt finning techniques that are appropriate for the local environment.
- [ ] An Emergency Action Plan (EAP) for every spring you dive.
- [ ] Primary and backup lights, if appropriate and permitted by local authorities.

Diver Statement: Any questions I answered incorrectly I've had explained to me and I understand what I missed.

Signature_____ Date_____

Quick Review – Spring Diver Answer Key

1. **What is spring diving?**
   - ☐ Diving during the spring equinox, also known as the vernal equinox.
   - ■ Scuba diving in any natural aquatic environment where fresh water flows from an aquifer to the earth's surface.
   - ☐ A water-entry technique where a diver bounces off the platform like a spring.
   - ☐ Diving in pool-like conditions.

2. **What is not an advantage of spring diving?**
   - ☐ Springs are often easily accessible by vehicle.
   - ☐ Spring diving is generally much less expensive than saltwater boat diving.
   - ■ There are many aquatic creatures in springs that can attack or hurt you.
   - ☐ Visibility tends to be superior.

3. **What are some concerns of spring diving?**
   - ■ Sections of some springs have overhead environments or access to them.
   - ■ The amount of outflow and inflow through vents and siphons.
   - ■ Dive etiquette and crowd control.
   - ■ Some springs have very silty bottoms.

4. **What are three broad elements of the groundwater system associated with springs?**
   - ■ A recharge area or areas.
   - ■ One or more discharge points.
   - ■ An aquifer.
   - ☐ Tidal flow caused by the lunar cycle.

Quick Review – Spring Diver Answer Key

5. **What is karst?**

   ■ A unique type of underground terrain created when soluble rocks such as limestone, dolomite and sandstone can filter or channel water.

   ☐ An aquatic grass often found in Australian springs.

   ☐ A type of specialized cave diving equipment.

   ☐ An impervious layer of rock or clay beneath the earth's surface.

6. **What is the average outflow of a 1st magnitude spring?**

   ■ 100 cubic ft/sec or 65 million gallons/day, or more.

   ☐ 75 cubic ft/sec or 45 million gallons/day.

   ☐ No more than 100 cubic ft/sec or 65 million gallons/day.

   ☐ The answer cannot be determined from the information given.

7. **What factors can affect the amount of water that discharges from springs?**

   ■ The size and composition of fissures within underground rocks.

   ■ The water pressure in the aquifer.

   ■ The amount of rainfall.

   ■ Groundwater withdrawals from agricultural or populated areas far away.

8. **You can't find your buddy in a dark and silty spring. What should you do?**

   ☐ Turn on your light and use it to look for your buddy.

   ☐ Begin a circular search pattern, making sure to stay off the bottom.

   ☐ Swim into the overhead environment and see if your buddy went there.

   ■ Follow standard safe diving procedures. Look for your buddy for no longer than one minute, then conduct a safe ascent and rejoin at the surface.

Quick Review – Spring Diver Answer Key

9. What is a halocline?

- ☐ A distinct layer in some springs where saltwater sits on top of fresh water.
- ■ A zone where a saltwater layer is trapped below a freshwater layer.
- ■ A unique feature of some springs near the ocean that can block sunlight.
- ☐ A temperature gradient in water where it changes from warm to cold.

10. What are the three types of spring diving?

- ■ Drift spring diving.
- ■ Shore spring diving.
- ☐ Thermal spring diving.
- ■ Boat spring diving.

11. What things should a good spring diver have?

- ■ Good buoyancy control.
- ■ No-silt finning techniques that are appropriate for the local environment.
- ■ An Emergency Action Plan (EAP) for every spring you dive.
- ■ Primary and backup lights, if appropriate and permitted by local authorities.

Diver Statement: Any questions I answered incorrectly I've had explained to me and I understand what I missed.

Signature_____   Date_____

Spring Diver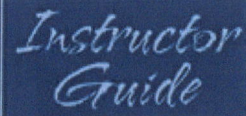

PADI Distinctive Specialty Training Record
Spring Diver

Instructor Statement:

"I verify that this student diver has satisfactorily completed all academic and/or any confined water training sessions as outlined in the PADI Distinctive Specialty Course Instructor Guide for Spring Diver. I am a renewed, Teaching status PADI Instructor in this Distinctive Specialty."

Instructor Name: _____ PADI # _____
Instructor Signature: _____ Completion Date: _____
                                                                                                             Day/Month/Year

Open Water Dive One

"I verify that this student diver has satisfactorily completed Dive One as outlined in the PADI standardized Distinctive Specialty Instructor Guide for Spring Diver, including:

- Plan and execute a spring dive appropriate to local conditions and topography
- Effective entry, exit, descent, no-silt finning, hovering, and buoyancy control while exploring a freshwater spring environment
- Safe and appropriate techniques before, during and after a spring dive

I am a renewed, Teaching status PADI Instructor in this Distinctive Specialty."

Instructor Name: _____ PADI # _____
Instructor Signature: _____ Completion Date: __+_____
                                                                                                             Day/Month/Year

Open Water Dive Two

"I verify that this student diver has satisfactorily completed Dive One as outlined in the PADI standardized Distinctive Specialty Instructor Guide for Spring Diver, including:

- Plan and execute a spring dive appropriate to local conditions and topography
- Look for, identify and log specific features that characterize a particular spring, such as fossils, vents, siphons, aquatic plants, vertebrates and invertebrates
- Safe and appropriate techniques before, during and after a spring dive

I am a renewed, Teaching status PADI Instructor in this Distinctive Specialty."

Instructor Name: _____ PADI # _____
Instructor Signature: _____ Completion Date: _____
                                                                                                             Day/Month/Year

(continued on p.52)

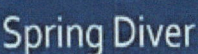 

(continued from p.51)

Student Diver Statement

"I verify that I have completed all performance requirements for this Spring Diver Distinctive Specialty. I am adequately prepared to dive in areas and under conditions similar to those in which I was trained. I agree to abide by PADI standard Safe Diving Practices."

Student Diver Name: _____

Student Diver Signature: _____ Completion Date:_____

                                                                                               Day/Month/Year

Spring Diver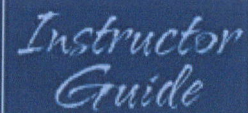

Copyright © 2018 by Edward Krawczyk and Edward Zellem.
All rights reserved.

www.ingramcontent.com/pod-product-compliance
Lightning Source LLC
Chambersburg PA
CBHW041547220426
43665CB00002B/51